Pearls Of Poetry

Sharon Bowman Griffin

Pearls of Poetry

Copyright © 2013 Sharon B. Griffin

All rights reserved.

ISBN: 0615943020
ISBN-13: 978-0615943022

DEDICATION

This is book is dedicated to my family, past and present who gave me the gifts of love, knowledge, pride and most importantly faith.

Pearls of Poetry

Pearls of Poetry

CONTENTS

God First — 7

Loving Feelings — 26

Special Occasions — 40

Food For Thought — 52

About The Author — 62

Pearls of Poetry

God First

Sharon B. Griffin

IN PRAISE OF GOD
God's love is beyond measure.
It's an everlasting, precious treasure!
It's higher than a mountain, deeper than the deepest sea;
For it, He gave His only Son and saved a wretch like me!

I cannot help but praise Him and glorify His name!
He's the Master of Creation; forever He shall reign!
It is my joy to serve Him, and seek to learn His ways.
Nothing have I done to earn it, but He blesses all my days!

When I think of His goodness, His tender, loving mercies,
I must humbly bow before Him and pray on bended knees.
He is my soul's salvation; He's the way, truth and the life!
He led my sin-sick soul out of darkness, into light!

Like a shepherd, He leads me; He's my Anchor and my Rock.
Lost and hungry, He feeds and guides me back to His flock.
He is Alpha and Omega - the Beginning and the End!
He is Comforter and Keeper; He is Father, Mother, Friend!

He is Lord of all in heaven, and on earth, in sky, in sea!
Lord of the whole universe, and yet, He watches over me!
He's my Comforter and Keeper, Provider and Healer, too.
He's my strength day by day; there is nothing I can't do!

I will worship Him forever; sing praises to Him alone;
I'll follow Him through this journey into my eternal home.
I'll lean on His everlasting arms for strength to run this race,
Until that great and glorious day I see Him, face to face!

A NATIONAL PRAYER
They that rule over us must be just.
Lord, give us leaders we can trust!
We are one nation under God;
yet, wrong paths sometimes we trod.

We do not always listen to You,
but do things we ought not to do.
Surely, the road that we now travel,
could cause our nation to unravel.

Help us to turn from wicked ways,
and become again, a nation that prays.
Give us discernment, Lord, and vision
so we can make Godly decisions.

We need leaders in times like these
who will help our burdens to ease.
Lord, give us wisdom to elect,
leaders who show You proper respect.

Order for us, our every step.
Then all nations will know we are kept
by the grace and mercy of our Master,
Almighty God, Who saves from disaster.

At the crossroads, now we stand.
Guide us by Your mighty hand.
In this world, let us be a beacon light…
…a nation that will do what's right!

America must represent
Your goodness in our government.
Only if we do the right thing,
can we loudly, proudly sing:

*"America, America, God shed His grace on thee,
and crown thy good with brotherhood
from sea to shining sea! "*

A PSALM OF PRAISE

You know the sorrows of my heart,
the longings of my soul
You've walked beside me from the start,
Your Hand, my hand doth hold.

Why You love such a worm as I,
I do not understand.
You rule the earth and reign on high,
the angels, You command.

Yet, this unworthy lump of clay,
You chose not to despise,
But became flesh to pave the way
for me to reach the skies.

You're the Great and Sovereign Lord,
with blessings, You anoint.
You are the Balm in Gilead,
when others disappoint.

You are the God of Israel
I worship and adore
You are the Precious, Worthy Lamb

I praise for evermore!

ASCRIBE TO MY HEART

Ascribe to my heart songs of faith, hope and love.
Bathe me with tender mercies from above.
Give me for utterance, a tongue full of praise.
Light up my spirit with Your blessed rays!

Grant me a voice, Lord, to lift up Your name.
By Your grace, let me help a lost soul to be claimed.
Ascribe to my heart, Lord, all of these things;
all these things, to my heart ascribe.

Ascribe to my heart, Lord, the spirit of Christ.
Show me what Your perfect will is for my life.
Appoint me a place in Your kingdom on high.
Fit me with wings, so to You, I can fly.

Hear me when my burdens, to You, Lord, I bring.
Deliver my soul, Lord, from death'cruel sting.
Ascribe to my heart, Lord, all of these things,
all these things, to my heart ascribe.

Sharon B. Griffin

CHRISTIAN LIVIN'

Lawd, Chrisjun' livin's takin' a toll on me.
It ain't as easy as I thought t'would be!
Gotta read mah Bible every day.
On top 'a dat, I still gotta pray!

Gotta make good 'cisions day and night
'T'ween what's wrong 'n what's right!
Cain't stay mad; mus'fo'git 'n fo'give...
It sho' ain't no easy life ta live!

Gotta try real hard ta be a saint...
...knowin' sho's you bo'n, I ain't!
Time flies by wit' a tick, tick, tick,
yet um s'posta fin' time ta visit de sick!

S'posta take the time ta say, "Hello."
'N ask, "Howdy do?" when I don't wanna kno'!
Hard 'nuf jes keepin' up wit' mahself,
but specs' me ta worry 'bout er'body else?

I praise You all week an' shout on Sunday,
eem' if I kin barely speak come Monday!
S'posta feed the po', but I ain't rich!
Cain't somebody feed me fo' a switch?

Gots me a closet full a clos' 'n cain't wear half o' 'em,
Oughta gi' some 'way, but Gawd, You knos I luv 'em!
'Sides, how um s'posta fin' time to share?
I gots ta git mah nails done an' mah hair!

Now, Lawd, what I'd really like ta do
is leeve all this stuff up ta You!
See, I kno's You do all things right;
'n me? I c'n have me some fun tonight!

(CHRISTIAN LIVIN' –CONT'D)

Aftah all, we only gits three score 'n ten
'befo' we pays the price fo' sin!
So I needs ta hurry and make has'e!
Dere ain't no time ta spare or was'e!

DRAW YE LIVING WATERS

Draw ye living waters from the well of salvation
Ye blessed sons and daughters of every tribe and nation.
They shall not hurt or destroy in all My holy mountain,
But drink the wine of joy from My never-ending fountain!

So travel ye the highway made for you by your God…
a pathway through steep waters, where ye may go dryshod.
Lift ye up, therefore, a banner…Almighty is He,
The Holy One of Israel, Who is in the midst of thee!

Sharon B. Griffin

ETERNAL REVELATION

Suddenly, joyously changed!
Unfettered, no longer tied down!
Oh, how deliciously strange,
is this new life I have found!

I feel myself floating on air,
no longer a slave to the night.
Your presence is everywhere,
Oh, what a wondrous delight!

You have put a song in my soul!
I dance like a leaf on the wind!
Like a blossom that slowly unfolds,
that is how this new life begins!

I hear sweet music, somehow,
falling, gently, on my ear.
Couldn't hear it before, but now,
it is perfectly, crystal clear!

Your Spirit overshadows me
and fills me with newness of life!
Now I shall forever be free
with my Savior, in paradise!

Transformed in the blink of an eye,
this one who was made from of dust!
Free at last, I truly can fly
on angel's wings, untrussed!

They eagerly wait to meet me…
…the elders, twenty and four!
They form a circle to greet me
with loved ones who've gone on before!

Joyous tears, like a flowing river,
Stream from my weeping eyes!

ETERNAL REVELATION (CONT'D)
For I behold the Him, the Giver
of this great gift of paradise!

He sits humbly before me!
I can see His nail-scarred feet and hands!
I feel so undone and unworthy,
but I sense that He understands.

I can't help approaching to Him quickly,
then I fall, prostrate, at His seat!
Tears of joy and sorrow fall swiftly.
They are washing over His feet!

He stands me before Him, gently;
looking fervently in my eyes.
"Well done, my faithful servant!
There is no need for you to cry.

You are my precious lamb!
I bled and died for you!
I wanted you here where I am!
By My grace, you have made it through!

We have slain a fatted calf
and prepared for you a great feast!
Rejoice! You are home at last!
You will live with us in peace!"

Next, He dried my flowing tears
and gave me a crown to wear.
He said, "Cast aside worries and fears!
My kingdom you shall share!"

Then a sacred crowd gathered around
as angels began to sing.
Four winged creatures bowed down,
Chanting, "Glory to our King!"

ETERNAL REVELATION (CONT'D)

The heavenly host worshiped as one
and then burst forth in song.
With joy, I rushed to be among
their everlasting throng!

I'll dance, shout, and twirl about!
I'll be happy beyond belief!
So shall it be, I have no doubt,
when my Savior, I shall meet!

I'VE MADE A VOW!

I've chosen to lead a Christian life,
to shun evil, and do what's right.
Promised I'd do the best I can
to love and care for my fellow man.
I've made a vow, and that's a fact.
I've made a vow, and I can't go back!

I've accepted Christ as Savior and Lord,
and eternal life as my reward.
I've left the world of sin, so dark.
I'm pressing on, toward the mark.
I've made a vow, and that's a fact.
I've made a vow and I can't go back!

I've told Him I would feed His sheep."
I made Him a promise that I must keep.
I've anchored my soul in His Holy word.
To turn back now, would be absurd!
I've made a vow, and that's a fact;
I'VE MADE A VOW, AND I CAN'T GO BACK !!

Sharon B. Griffin

I SAW YOU TODAY

I saw You today, a lush green carpet under my feet.
Your smell tickled my nose, and I sneezed!
Above, You wore blue with white accessories.
Below, You wore all the colors You pleased!

I felt Your lovely light warming me somehow,
And I felt Your kiss of moisture cooling my brow!
Your breath gently pressed at my back,
nudging me back onto the right track.

I heard You singing sweetly in the trees…
…such soft and soothing melodies!
I smiled as You buzzed past my ear
to attend a flower, blooming near.

I tasted Your goodness from a tiny stream.
It was pure, invigorating and serene!
I tasted Your honey, sticky and sweet,
my gnawing hunger to defeat!

I even saw You watching over me tonight,
twinkling overhead and shining bright!
Felt You closing my eyes in peaceful sleep,
my heart knowing Your love for me is deep!

KEEP MOVING UP !

When I was a child, I struggled to stand,
and I did…with the aid of helping hands!
As I grew, I learned how to walk and run…
to keep moving up toward the light of the Son!

Through my troubling teens, times were tough,
But a Helper unseen kept me moving up!
Soon, I came to see that I was not alone,
that I was not climbing all on my own!

Others were there on the slippery slopes.
Some were even trying to show me the ropes,
to teach me what to do and what not,
to point me toward the Solid Rock!

Heavy rains or strong winds may knock me down,
but I keep moving up, seeking higher ground!
My grip's growing stronger across the years,
despite cuts and bruises, despite many tears!

I press toward the mark, my goal is the prize
above heavenly clouds and earthly skies.
If, by Grace, you're climbing, too,
please help me, and I'll help you!

Together, we will reach the top
if we keep climbing and do not stop;
if we grip Solid Rock, not shifting sands;
if we put our lives in Omnipotent Hands.

If we keep on climbing, keep moving up,
then with eternal blessings, He will fill our cup!

Sharon B. Griffin

YOU ARE MY SANCTUARY

You are my special place!
You make me feel warm and safe!
I have no fear of hurt or harm
within the shelter of Your arms.

You are my valley of peace!
In Your presence, my soul's at ease!
Problems flee and troubles fade
beneath Your cool and pleasant shade.

You are my mountain high!
You soar my spirits to the sky!
No greater joy have I found
than standing on Your Holy ground.

You are my calming sea!
You gently rock and cradle me!
Protecting, like a mother's womb,
You soothe me like a sacred tune.

YOU ARE MY SANCTUARY!

POWERS AND PRINCIPALITIES

The shooter poised, steadied his aim, and fired!
They began to fall...first one, then another, then hundreds...thousands... millions!!
Many tried to escape, but just when they thought they were safe - BAMMMM!

The shooter's lips pealed back in a smug, self-satisfied smile.
His attack went better than anticipated! Some actually ran toward the path of destruction.
Others unwittingly stumbled into their fate; still others fought futilely to escape!
They were all doomed. Like lost sheep, he decimated them, one by one! If he had to pay, so would they!
Soon and very soon, he would kill them all!

Meanwhile, an emergency meeting of the Highest Authorities convened inutmost secrecy. The enemy must be stopped, they all agreed. A covert plan was
formulated to outwit him! It was ingenious, challenging, and required perfect execution!
The shooter must not know until it was too late, that he had been out maneuvered.
The Son volunteered for the dangerous, four-part mission.
He entered the dead zone without fanfare, clothed in helpless humanity.
The shooter shuddered with a sudden sense of foreboding.
He sent henchmen searching for an intruder, but to no avail.

The Son grew quickly, increasing in knowledge and wisdom, preparing Himself to do battle!
He healed the sick, re-acquainted them with the source of their healing, and showed them
how to heal themselves and others.
His fame spread abroad, until one day
the shooter had Him in his site at last!
The shooter tried unsuccessfully to exploit Him.

Sharon B. Griffin

POWERS AND PRINCIPALITIES(CONT'D)

But the Son was much stronger than the shooter thought!
For the time being, the shooter shifted aim and resumed
attacking the weaker prey.
Then the Son shielded the intended victims
with His Own Body!
He cleansed their wounds with His Blood.
"This Way, I will save you!" He urged.
Those who heard and obeyed, He shielded from death,
giving up His Own Life!

The Son even descended to the depths of hell,
to defeat the shooter there!
He wrested from him, the keys to death
and to life everlasting!

Then, He raised Himself up and ascended
triumphantly to the heights of glory!
There, He celebrated His coup with the Highest Authorities,
and began preparations for His return to planet earth, to
claim complete and final victory over the shooter.

Until then, an Unseen Emissary would guide, protect and
comfort His precious sheep!
Knowing his fate is sealed, but unwilling to admit defeat, the
shooter slowly begins to fall..
.but he keeps on firing, Firing, FIRING... to the bitter end!

OH THAT HOLY, HOLY MOUNTAIN

Oh, that holy, holy mountain,
where God made His presence known!
When the bush was set on fire,
and His wondrous glory shown.

My how fear and fascination grip me,
At this curious sight that I behold:
A bush, afire yet not burning
but talking…what a wonder to my soul!

Moses, quick, remove your sandals,
Even though you are spellbound,
Here, My Pure Spirit burns eternal,
and where you are standing is holy ground!

Oh, that holy, holy mountain,
where God made His presence known!
When the bush was set on fire,
and His wondrous glory shown.

Master, I prostrate myself before You.
Your Radiance makes blush with shame!
Lord, have mercy; don't destroy me.
Pray tell me, what is Your Name?

I am that I am, servant, Moses.
Say I am the Great I Am,
God of Abraham, Isaac and Jacob,
I led you 'cross the burning sand!

Oh, that holy, holy mountain,
where God made His presence known!
When the bush was set on fire,
and His wondrous glory shown.

Sharon B. Griffin

OH THAT HOLY, HOLY MOUNTAIN (CONT'D)

Truly, I am Your humble servant.
Lord, what would You have me do?
Surely, You know I am not worthy.
Still, I'll do my best for You.

Go whither I send thee, Moses.
I shall set My people free.
You're the one that I have chosen
lead My sheep to liberty…

Oh, that holy, holy mountain,
where God made His presence known!
When the bush was set on fire,
and His wondrous glory shown!

YOU'RE ALWAYS THERE

You're always there, You're always there…
Showing me how much You care;
You comfort me in my despair,
You're always there!

You're always there, You're always there…
You pick me up and fill my cup,
You always give more than enough,
You're always there!

You're always there, You're always there…
You're sunshine in the midst of rain;
You're the rainbow that keeps me sane,
If I but call on Your name, You're always there!

You're always there, You're always there…
You're my joy, You're my song;
You forgive when I do wrong,
It's to You, I belong; You're always there!

You're always there, You're always there…
You always hear my anxious prayer;
Your love, You never fail to share….
You're ALWAYS THERE!

Loving Feelings

A LOVE AFFAIR

I met the love of my life when I was barely 6 years old!
My teacher introduced us; Imagine that!!!
It was love at first sight. One look, and I was hooked!
His name was, Dic Tionary.
He was everything I ever wanted, and more!

We grew closer as the years rolled by!
We went steady in high school and most of college.
For a while, though I got distracted.
See, I met this guy known as The Saurus.
He turned my head, and we became an item!

So many wanted him, I knew he'd never be just mine!
I finally decided we should just be friends,
and I returned to my true love.
Dic Tionary took me back and we got married!

Together, we've produced lots of offspring!
Seems like every time we look at each other,
along comes another one!
I think we're going to grow old together!
ISN'T LOVE GRAND?

Sharon B. Griffin

A PARADOX

How can it be, that I am in you and you in me?
A love so true: one heart, beating for two.
Separate but equal parts of one whole…1 heart, 1 soul
connected, respected, completely affected,
trying to be cool, calm, and collected!

Why is it so that the closer we get, the further we go
to battle against mighty waves of emotion?
Like salmon, swimming upstream in the ocean,
We're fighting a battle that's already won!
Defeated but unwilling to quit; unable to admit

that love does, indeed, conquer all!
The harder you fight, the harder you fall!
We're wishing and hoping there'll come a day
somehow, somewhere, sometime, some way
to resolve the pregnant mystery
of love that grows where it should not be!

AN AFFAIR OF THE HEART

Who can control an affair of the heart?
When did it begin? Where did it start?
Will it lead bring happiness or disaster?
Who really lives happily ever after?

You're held fast in a love-spun web,
Where deep emotions rise and ebb,
Where all efforts to wiggle free
move you closer to your destiny.

Riding in the eye of the hurricane,
fearing things may never be the same,
you pray that better days will come,
if not for you, then for someone.

Things are immaterial to happiness,
A poor substitute they are, at best!
Mere things can never pass the test
That determines heart healthiness.

That answer lies only in you.
Deep inside, you know that's true!
So, Dr. Feelgood, heal thyself.
Otherwise, you'll kill yourself!

It's YOUR Choice!

BE PATIENT AND WAIT

The current between us flows so strong!
But, we do know right from wrong!
It's not our aim to cause each other pain,
Yet, love is useless when it is in vain.

We are trapped; caught in a "catch 22,"
neither one of us knowing just what to do,
and only God will determine our fate;
so all we can do, is be patient and WAIT!

CAUGHT AGAIN

I thought sure I'd hid myself far away from love,
But it hasn't taken much to prove how wrong I was!
For when I look into your eyes, it's staring back at me;
And I must confess, I guess, it's a welcome sight to see!

Won't do anything about it, no, I really wouldn't dare!
It wouldn't be too wise of me to show how much I care.
I sure wish I could run and hide again behind that wall
I built to shield my tender heart from such a nasty fall.

But it's too late, now, because the wall has tumbled down!
And I don't know if that should make me laugh or make me frown.
You are my joy and sorrow, which is quite a paradox;
You found the key and opened me, and now I am unlocked!

So here I am, caught again in love's merciless grip,
And hoping it won't prove to be too painful trip!

DO YOU QUALIFY?

Sure I'm glad you dig my body!
But, if you think that's all of me, not hardly!
You may believe my body is where it's at,
but there's much more to me than that!

Now, if you will seek, then you will find
a very fascinating and intelligent mind!
Don't get me wrong, I'm glad I'm blessed
with wealthy hips and an abundant chest!

Yes, I possess a warm smile and sexy walk,
sensuous style and slightly flirtatious talk.
Still, it's good conversation that turns me on!
We can communicate from dusk to dawn!

So if you want to show me a real good time,
don't just love my body, love my mind!
Both body and mind must be satisfied.
Good love and conversation must be supplied!

Are you up to the challenge? I know I am!
I don't want no "slam bam, thank you mam!"
If you step to me, you need to come correct;
that's the only way you'll earn my respect!

Wonder if I'm worth it? You better believe it!
The only question is: can you achieve it?
I have high standards…more than a few.
You must meet or beat them, to "do the do!"

I'm just telling you like it T- I-, TIS!
To be with me, you've got to mind your 'biz!
Yes, the mission is hard, but it's possible too!
Whether you take it or leave it, that's up to you!

Sharon B. Griffin

FEEL MY LOVE

Feel my love when we're apart
Growing deeper in your heart.
Feel my need, when you're not near
to hold you close to me, my dear.

Feel my fear of circumstance,
my hesitance to take a chance.
Feel my instinct to protect
and treat you with utmost respect.

Feel my passion, deep within
boiling, sometimes, to the brim.
Feel my hope that there might be
some day, a time for you and me.

HOLD MY HEART

Hold my heart like a fragile bird.
Please don't break its wings!
Help it soar above the clouds
as soft melodies, it sings.

Let my wounded spirit mend.
Soft tissues have been torn!
With harshness, do not offend.
Let tenderness adorn!

Be patient with the kid in me.
She just needs time to grow.
Help her to be all she can be;
If not, she'll never know!

Open my eyes so I can see
The things I can't envision.
Encourage me to conceive
a new and greater vision!

Hold my hand; don't let go
or I may fall apart!
You are the best part of me
and have been, from the start!

INTO TO LOVE 101

I. **DEFINITIONS**
   A. When the feeling's so filling, you can barely breathe around it.
   B. When you feel something vital was lost, but you've suddenly found it.
   C. When the one you love comes in view, and all others fade from it.
   D. When your soul sings your favorite love song, and your heart seems to drum it.

II. **SYMPTOMS**
   A. Your eye-hand coordination is definitely shot!
   B. Your speech and movement is shaky at the start.
   C. If your love isn't with you, you slowly fall apart,
   D. And happy holidays become hollow days in your heart.

III. **EFFECTS**
   A. You find you've become an emotional roller coaster!
   B. The thought of your love makes you feel as warm as a toaster!
   C. Suddenly, somehow, your life seems incredibly sweet.
   D. You finally feel that you have been made complete.

IV. **TREATMENT/CURE**
   A. If the love that you're feeling is true and pure, you'll find that there really isn't a cure.
   B. But even though it's a fatal disease, you'll find that it's also one with which you'll be pleased.
   C. So treat your love like the treasure it is, and forget about finding cures, because, gee whiz:
   D. If you choose to make the most of it while you can; you'll find it's the most desirable disease known to man.

KEEPING THE FAITH

Keeping the faith that your heart is with me,
for surely you know, that mine is with thee.
If it were not so, it could not have hurt me
so deeply to think that you would desert me.

Keeping the faith in a love so strong
that it redefines what is right and what's wrong;
that it holds us captive, but prisoners so willing
to be bound by the irresistible feeling!

Keeping the faith in a love so true,
that nothing and no one else will do.
Keeping the faith in a love so pure
that it struggles, against the odds, to endure.

Keeping the faith, and trusting in us
to survive even when the going gets tough.
Keeping the faith, amid challenges great and small.
Keeping the faith that love does indeed conquer all!

Sharon B. Griffin

LET ME LOVE
(Based on 1 Corinthinans 13)

Let me love with an unselfish love,
that from beginning to end
seeks not to benefit itself, but to be the truest friend.
A love that encourages, that does not hurt or destroy,
a love that helps, a love that heals, a love that produces joy.

Let me love with a Christ-like love, one that suffers long,
that past hurts remembers not; keeps no record of wrongs.
A love that soothes, a love that heals,
that strengthens and preserves
the things in life that matter most,
things every heart deserves.

Let me love with an un-controlling love
that does not manipulate;
that seeks no glorify for itself, nor belittles or berates.
A love that seeks to set souls free,
rather than hold them back
A love that only aspires to be whatever others lack.

Let me love with a love as new as dawn,
as peaceful as sunset,
a love as solid as the ground, as high as the sky can get.
A love that will always cherish, a love that is pure as gold,
a love that will never perish, a love that will never grow old.

O let me love as I am loved by the One Who created me,
for His love is perfect love, no greater love can there be.
Let me love as He does love; forgive, for I am forgiven.
O let my love reflect His love, and take me home to heaven!

LITTLE STOLEN MOMENTS

Little, stolen moments...
capsules of time...
snatched here and there
for two hearts to share.

Little stolen moments...
how quickly they pass...
precious, but fleeting,
doomed not to last.

Little stolen moments...
they come and they go...
to a place in the heart
only two can know.

Little stolen moments...
capsules of time...
gone with the wind,
except from the mind.

OPEN

Open the door shut long ago,
trapping your soul in its sorrow.
Free your mind from its prison of pain.
Open your heart and live again!

Break down your barrier of false pride.
Allow true love to come inside.
Remove your mask, and feelings share.
Open your eyes; there are others who care.

Tear down your wall of phony pretense
so others may come to your defense!
OPEN! For it is only then
pain can go out, and love can come in!

Sharon B. Griffin

THE KISS

From nowhere came an unexpected, delightful intrusion,
like a cool breeze on a steamy summer night;
or the melodic rustle of leaves on a crisp autumn day!
Gentle…tentative…like a child's awkward first steps,
then bolder, exploring…forging past forbidden barriers.

The foundation of my will collapsed!
I was swept away, suspended on a cloud of ecstasy,
past realms of reality to where my spirit soared free,
yet was captive to the iron grip of emotion.

A damn broke inside of me, feelings flooded my being
A million colors, with eyes wide shut, I was seeing.
Time stood still, but, clearly, the earth moved!
My heart leaped for joy…and then I woke up!

WHEN LOVE DIES

Where does love go to die?
Where does the graveyard of broken hearts lie?
Who lingers there in grief to mourn
the unbeating heart, shattered and torn?
Whose duty is making the fatal announcement:
"Time of death, unknown", the final pronouncement?
What unseen headstone marks the lowly tomb
of love's spirit when it returns to earth's womb?

What trace is there of skeletal remains
bearing witness to love's suffering and pain?
Who preaches a love's final eulogy?
Who sings a love's solemn elegy?
And, when a love's passing is complete
does the pulse of the world ever skip a beat?
Who acknowledges its exit and cries
at so great a loss as when love dies?

Sharon B. Griffin

Special Ocassions

A TURKEY OF A POEM

I used to be so proud!
I had a royal strut.
I gobbled long and loud;
didn't know I was in a rut!
Why, all the people love me!
(At least, that's what I thought,
until I learned my destiny
was to be killed and bought!)

Sharon B. Griffin

CHRISTMAS JOY

Our Prince of Peace lay in a cradle of hay.
Joy entered to the world on Christmas Day!
The Baby Divine, God's promise of old.
was born in a manger, as long foretold.

While angels sang and kings bowed down,
our Great King slept, with glory around.
They spread the good news; shared the great tiding
that Our Savior and Lord, with us was abiding!

Our world was full of darkness and woe,
'til the Christ Child brought us salvation and hope!
Gold, myrrh, and frankincense sweet…
all manner of gifts wise men laid at His feet.

Yet, not for material things, did He come.
He purposed to save all mankind…every one!
A miracle it was that a tiny Child,
one day, God and man would reconcile!

Amazing grace, He offered to all…
a gift so great in a package so small!
Emanuel - God with us in human flesh,
to pardon our sin and forgive our trespass!

O come and let us adore Him today!
He Who was born, our sin debts to pay!
Christmas Day, ever holy and blessed one
when God gave the world the gift of His Son.

FAMILY AND FRIENDS

It's so good to be here, so good to see,
Wonderful friends and dear family.
Far better than silver, more precious than gold
Are the memories we share from our days of old.

A room full of laughter, a room full of fun,
A room full of good will towards everyone;
No matter the wind, no matter the weather,
Our friendships and kinships have brought us together.

I look in your eyes, and what I do I see
But the love of Christ Jesus reflecting on me;
So whereever life leads, be it near or far
Remember how precious each one of you are.

Eat, drink, and be merry--but remember the reason:
We celebrate in this Holy season.
Attend to your hunger, attend to your thirst,
Attend to your needs, but please put Christ first.

May this sweet reunion be the start of many,
May the joys that we share be often and plenty.
May each new generation blossom and flourish
Like fragrant flowers forever to cherish!

Let's thank God our Father every day
For the abundant blessings He sends our way
And for the greatest gift we've received from above--
The gift of our Savior and His selfless love!

Written for the Celebration of Family and Friends

Sharon B. Griffin

GATHERED AT THE TABLE

The first day of the Feast of Unleavened bread
The Passover Lamb, to His disciples, said:
"One of you who sups with Me,
shall soon betray Me, verily."

Nearly every heart became heavy gloom
as they fellowshipped in the Upper Room.
One by one, each asked, "Is it I?"
All but one, thinking, "Why Lord, why?'

Jesus gave thanks as He broke bread.
Then, to His beloved disciples, He said:
"This is My body, take it and eat.
Drink this wine for My blood, to complete."

"It is poured out for many, so do not be sad.
Enjoy this fellowship with Me, and be glad.
For I will not again share this cup with you,
'til in My Father's kingdom, I drink it anew."

Peter brooded, "Master, I tell You no lie,
I will not betray You, even if I die!"
Jesus answered, "Before the cock crows thrice,
My dear friend, Peter, you will deny Me twice!"

"Nevertheless, I will complete My mission.
Before you, I will go, after I have risen
I will meet you again, in Galilee.
Then, you'll take up your cross, and follow Me!"

HOLY NIGHT SO CELEBRATED

Oh night, holy night so long awaited,
Oh night, holy night so celebrated:

A quiet hush fell across the land
as angels heralded God's gift to man.
A great star appeared in the Eastern sky
to show that the birth of the Christ Child was nigh.

Wise men with gold, frankincense and myrrh,
came to worship Him and honor His birth.
The light of that star was their constant guide.
It led them right to the sweet Baby's side.

Shepherds quaked, and cattle were lowing.
through the night, as cold winds were blowing
while in a manger, lined only with hay,
Baby Jesus, the light of the world, did lay.

Oh night, holy night so long awaited,
Oh night, holy night so celebrated:

Mary and Joseph, with wonder and joy,
gave thanks to the Lord for their dear Baby Boy.
And their Infant Divine, without one little peep,
wrapped in swaddling clothes, lay fast asleep.

Little Lord Jesus, the Almighty King ,
salvation and hope to this world would bring!
In humblest of circumstances was He born.
He wore no crown, or jewels to adorn.

He was born to bear an unmerited cross,
to heal the sick and to search for the lost!
He was born for all of mankind's rescue;
Savior of the world, most men never knew!

Sharon B. Griffin

(HOLY NIGHT SO CELEBRATED-CON'TD)

Oh night, holy night so long awaited,
Oh night, holy night so celebrated:

Oh night, holy night, when heaven smiled
Oh night when God sent His only Child
to save us from a cruel but just fate...
Oh night of great love, we celebrate!
Oh holy night of our dear Savior's birth,
Oh precious night of unspeakable worth!

Oh night we acknowledge so that all may know
how deeply and selflessly He loves us all so!
How that night, God, in man manifest,
the kingdoms of this world has blest!
The sting of death we bear no more!
O come, let us worship Him and adore!

Oh night, holy night so long awaited,
Oh night, holy night so celebrated:

Joy to the world, the Lord is come,
Bow down and worship Him, every one!
Rejoice and be glad! God's praises sing!
Our Savior is born; reign forever, Great King!

HOSANNA ! HOSANNA! LET GOD ARISE
(in honor of Glenn Burleigh's Cantata, "Let God Arise")

Hosanna! Hosanna! Let God arise!
His praises sing to the listening skies!
He's the Heir of Salvation; in Him victory lies.
Let God, let God arise!

He conquered the grave; His enemies scattered!
From death, He saves; its sting He shatters!
Rejoice! Rejoice! He answers our cries.
Let God, let God arise!

Christ is the Worthy Lamb that was slain!
He laid down His life, only to reclaim!
Hail the King of Kings and Savior of lives!
Let God, let God arise!

The battle is over; it's finished; it's done!
He arose from the grave; the victory is won!
Come let us adore Him, Who won the prize!
Let God, let God arise!

Hosanna! Hosanna! Let God arise!
He is all powerful, wonderful and wise!
Eternal life, He alone supplies!
Let God, let God arise!

Sharon B. Griffin

THANKFUL THOUGHTS

Today, Lord, I am thankful.
I am thankful for the life you've given me.
I am thankful that you set my spirit free.
I am thankful that my Savior died for me.

Today, Lord, I am thankful.
I am thankful for the birds that sweetly sing.
I am thankful for the showers in the spring.
I am thankful, Lord, for every living thing.

Today, Lord, I am thankful.
I am thankful for the grass and sparkling dew.
I am thankful for my family, and friends, too.
I am thankful for trials You brought me through.

Today, Lord, I am thankful.
I am thankful for the moon and stars above.
I am thankful for Your sacrifice of love.
I am thankful for children I'm so proud of.

Today, Lord, I am thankful.
I am thankful for I have been richly blessed.
I am thankful for I feel such happiness.
I am thankful for me, You gave YOUR VERY BEST.

EVERY DAY, LORD, I AM THANKFUL!

THE CROSS

I must've felt like the weight of the world
placed upon His back,
pressing in to His torn open skin, 'til His body,
with pain, was racked!
I felt Him tremble beneath my bulk, as
He lifted me up the hill;
Twice, He fell, but rose again, to do His Father's will.

I would have flung myself away, if only...if only I could!
But, I could not, for I was just a lifeless piece of wood!
They drove me hard into the ground
and nailed Him on to me;
I was a woeful witness to His pain and agony.

I thought, 'I wish that I had hands to wipe His sweaty brow,
For those who do, laugh and dance and spit upon Him now!'
"It is for you," I longed to scream, "that He is hanging here!"
Even if my wooden mouth could speak,
would they shed a tear?

They were so busy having fun at their Savior's expense,
while He slowly bled and died, for their recompense.
When, at last, they took Him down,
the earth began to quake.
Thunder roared so very loud, some sleeping souls did wake!

And, as I tumbled to the ground, my shameful duty done,
the crowd, who'd cast lots for His shroud,
in panic, began to run!
I lay there, separated from Him, in the rain-soaked sod;
my wooden wounds weeping water for the Lamb of God!

Silently, He whispered to me, "The victory is won!
In just two days, you will see the rising of the Son!"
Then I knew my purpose, which I had not understood!
I was the Cross of Calvary, NOT just a piece of wood!

Sharon B. Griffin

THROUGH MY LITTLE EYES

I see you, sweet Jesus, through my little eyes,
hanging there on the cross, while my little heart cries.
How can people so foolish, think they're so wise?
I wish they could see You, through my little eyes!

Jesus, I still remember that day
they sent us away, but You said, "Let them stay!"
Then You blessed me, and scooped me up in Your arms…
I can't understand why they're doing You harm!

Why do they beat and tease You, spit in Your face?
Why won't You get down from that terrible place?
Jesus, why did they pick You to hate and despise?
I sure wish they could see You through my little eyes!

I see You, dear Jesus, as kind as can be,
I see You as the One Who truly loves me!
I don't understand; I don't want You to die!
How I wish they could see You through my little eyes!

YOU MAKE ME SMILE
(For Someone Special on Valentine's Day)

When I think of you, I get a warm fuzzy feeling,
because your friendship is so appealing!
It's not that easy to find someone,
with whom you can relax and have fun.

It's plain to see that you're my cup of tea.
You have such a pleasing personality.
I do hope we stay friends for quite a while.
Why is that? Because you make me smile!

Friendships come and friendships go,
That is a fact, and this I know.
But, yours is one I'd like to keep!
Maybe it will grow into something deep.

I ain't trying to push, but I'm keeping it real,
and I wanted you to know just how I feel.
It's Valentine's Day, so I'm taking a while
just to let you know…you make me smile

Sharon B. Griffin

Food For Thought

A BLACK PEARL

A Black pearl…unpolished, unrefined…
…waiting to be noticed, waiting to be shined…
…waiting to be freed from her lonely shell…
…waiting for someone to break the dark spell…

…waiting in anguish as time marches on…
…waiting, anticipating the dawn…
…waiting in vain for impossible dreams…
…waiting, but coming apart at the seams…

…waiting, her ebony sheen growing dimmer…
…waiting, watching as chances grow slimmer.
A Black pearl, unpolished, unrefined,
waiting, by love, to be redesigned!

Sharon B. Griffin

A CALLOUSED SOUL

Done killed you dead! What have I done?
You was too much like Massah, son!
An' you ain't show me no respec'
!You's goin' hit me; what'd you spec'?

You know, son, what really made me mad
was how much you look like your dad!
Dat white skin, blon' hair, n' pale blue eyes…
…dem cold, cruel eyes that I despise!

Lawd knows, son, I curse the day
dat blue-eyed devil came my way!
He forced himself on me, 'tis true!
See, son, that's why I hated you!

Because of you, I couldn't forgit.
I never could get over it!
I tried, though, son, I really tried
but, when I suckled you, I cried!

In my heart, yo' daddy made a hole
and it formed dis callous on my soul!
He stripped me of my sense of pride...
I think that was the day I died!

Still, son, I tried to carry on,
Still worked my fingers to de bone!
Still did what I was told to do
and still, inside, dat callous grew!

So I gave you money, a car and such,
to take de place o' yo' mama's touch!
I jes couldn't give you what you needed,
      no matta' how you begged and pleaded!

A CALLOUSED SOUL(CONT'D)

Son…you walked like him; you talked like him!
You even held your fork like him!...
An' here you was gon' beat me, too?
Das sumthin' I couldn' let you do!

'Sides, now, son, you's jes' like me. …
…'cept at lease you is at peace!
Son, you's bettah buried in dis hole
where no callous kin' grow on your soul!

Sharon B. Griffin

CHANCES

Like petals in the wind, they come and go.
Like ocean tides, they ebb and flow.
Chances can be given or made.
They can bloom, or they can fade.

They can come any time or any place!
If not acted upon, they soon erase.
They can be fickle, false, and fleeting…
…difficult, daunting, even defeating.

Chances can come once in a lifetime,
or in subtle layers that build and climb.
Like rainbows, chances have shades and hues.
Most come only after you've paid some dues.

They are like a book with an unturned page,
or a jackpot awaiting the right bet to be waged!
They're like victories won when a coin is tossed;
or like lines in the sand which were never crossed.

Chances often depend on life's circumstances.
They can have nuances, like great romances.
These things I know; therefore, my stance is:
In order to grow, you must take chances!

DAWN OF CREATION

Progenitor of genius, beauty and color;

from the beginning, present with God

and obedient to His will and purpose.

Behold the vessel wherein all is stored:

Look beyond the door, and see!

Sharon B. Griffin

A DREAM DIVERTED

Come and dream a dream with me
about the way things used to be:

The sky was blue, the air was clean.
Trees bore fruit, and grass was green.
No acid rain, no air pollution...
...no ozone threat with no solution.
No fish full of mercury.
No oil slicks on the open sea.
We had not heard of "El Nino."
Ice cream could be made from snow!

Our youth were sweet and innocent,
Time with family was well spent.
Doors lay open night and day.
The streets were safe for kids to play.
Violence as seldom used,
or children beaten and abused.
All our elders were respected.
Precious pets were not neglected.

How did we divert the dream
into the nightmare it now seems?
Hopefully, it's not too late
to waken from this altered state!
We need to have a change of heart,
before our world is torn apart!
The dream, somehow, must be restored
and made to last, forevermore.

DREAMS DEFERRED

Dreams deferred shrivel like grapes on the vine,
never yielding their sweetness to juice or to wine;
languishing in the netherworld of could have been,
they grow old, forgotten, withered and dim.
Dreams deferred crumble to the dust,
most likely unable to regain their thrust.
Because, if their time is allowed to pass,
they eventually give up the ghost, alas!

Jesus died for our sins, but not for our dreams.
Those, we must save ourselves, it seems.
For them, we must make our own sacrifice...
step out on our faith, and pay the price!
Dreams deferred cannot survive.
They cannot linger, more dead than alive.
Now is their moment; their acceptable time,
lest they die while trying to bud on the vine!

Sharon B. Griffin

DREAMING IMPOSSIBLE DREAMS

Dreams deferred shrivel like grapes on the vine,
never yielding their sweetness to juice or to wine;
languishing in the netherworld of could have been,
they grow old, forgotten, withered and dim.
Dreams deferred crumble to the dust,
most likely unable to regain their thrust.
Because, if their time is allowed to pass,
they eventually give up the ghost, alas!

Jesus died for our sins, but not for our dreams.
Those, we must save ourselves, it seems.
For them, we must make our own sacrifice...
step out on our faith, and pay the price!
Dreams deferred cannot survive.
They cannot linger, more dead than alive.
Now is their moment; their acceptable time,
lest they die while trying to bud on the vine!

I WRITE

I write the dictates of my heart,
I write the longings of my soul;
I write the struggles of the past,
I write the hope the future holds.
    I write...I write!

I write the puzzling things of life;
I write the things I understand.
I write the nuances of the night,
I write the language of the land!
    I write...I write!

I write the song of sweet romance,
I write the dirge when out of tune;
I write of joy and sorrow's dance.
I write the blueness of the moon!
    I write...I write!

I write the smell of baby's breath;
I write the creak of ancient knees...
I write the rhyme of birth and death;
I write the whispers of the trees.
    I write...I write!

I write of family and of friends;
I write of mysteries of the mind.
I write the way a story ends;
I write of ever-marching time.
    I write...I write!

I write of universal themes;
I write of the drummer's beat.
I write of the wildest dreams;
I write of summer's sweltering heat.
    I write...I write!

I write, I write, I write non-stop!
I write until my pencil drops!
I write...it's all I have to give;
I write, I write, I write to live.

ABOUT THE AUTHOR

Sharon Adele Bowman-Griffin was born and reared in Hampton, Virginia, the sixth child of Nathaniel Earl, Sr. and Josephine Purdy Bowman. Her interest in written expression began in pre-school and progressed into adulthood.

She entered and won her first poetry contest at age 14, and penned her junior high school alma mater! At the encouragement of family, friends and educators, she began to hone her literary skills..

She is a regular contributor to Ancestral Rites, a publisher of poetry by African American writers. The author holds membership in the Kinship of Authors writers' group..

A versatile and prolific writer, she also writes plays, short stories, has written a novel (unpublished at this time) and is writing a series of children's books.

The muse has also led the author to pursue song writing and compiling original gospel songs and hymns for publication. She considers her wonderful gift for written expression to be a blessing from God!

Ms Griffin also works to encourage other artists to actively pursue their dreams.

www.ingramcontent.com/pod-product-compliance
Lightning Source LLC
Chambersburg PA
CBHW061250040426
42444CB00010B/2341